GROW

In

Difficult Places

Learning to See Beauty Beyond the Dark

Jonas Nguh, PhD

RELENTLESS
PUBLIS-ING

Grow In Difficult Places : Learning to See Beauty Beyond the Dark

Copyright © 2019 by Jonah Nguh, Ph.D.

Published by :

Relentless Publishing House, LLC

RELENTLESS
PUBLIS-NG

www.relentlesspublishing.com

ISBN: 978-1-948829-311

First Edition : August 2019

10 9 8 7 6 5 4 3 2 1

Table of Contents

PREFACE

In a training session that I attended several years ago, the facilitator asked the group the following question: "WHEN HAVE YOU FELT MOST ALIVE? One answer from a team member caught me off guard: "When I was 15 and lost my best friend to leukemia." How could the devastating loss of a friend leave anyone feeling "alive"? Several years later during a Q& A session with a renowned healthcare executive, an audience member asked the keynote speaker, "WHAT HELPED PREPARE YOU TO BE SO SUCCESSFUL." THIS GOT AN EQUALLY surprising answer. The executive said this: "When I was fired from my job and had to move to another state. My world was crushed."

I can think of few things more difficult than losing a loved one or the loss of a career that one has worked hard to build for many years. But as the above answers demonstrate, I have learned that painful experiences can be an important part of preparing one for their own unique and beautiful journey personally and professionally. As humans it is only natural that we grow to be pain-averse. However, if we take an objective look and consider what causes human beings to develop, to grow and become our best selves, we find that people grow the most through adversity.

Our human tendency is to avoid or run away from difficult times and places. Difficulty often leads to a path of growth.

From an early age, I have had my fair share of difficulty; from illness and death of a loved one, disappointment to financial hardships. I have also experienced the warmth and comfort of family and friends who love me, to having the support of peers and mentors that encourage my hopes and dreams. As a child I experienced the love of parents who walked with me through my pain, experienced the love of a family that was always there and able to help me. I have also learned that having help does not negate taking action in our own lives.

As I grew up into young adulthood, I encountered different sorts of pain that make adulthood challenging. While the wounds from society are often invisible, they can hurt more: a friend's desertion, a denied opportunity, a teacher who says you will never amount to anything. Today, I stand on the other side strong with many lessons being learned. And that is what I hope to share with you in this book. From dealing with failure (*The Joy of Rejection*), to my naivety as an early careerist (*In Praise of Naivety*), to the importance of being authentic (*Finding Strength in Being Vulnerable*), to dealing with depression (*The Paradox of Success*); yes, we all have some issue we are dealing with, no one gets off easy! To my feelings of being a phony (*Ever Felt Like a Phony? Why Feeling Like a Fraud Can Be A Good Thing*).

My hope is to share with you some lessons learned through my unique journey that has often been in difficult places so that the reader realizes and believes that beauty often is found in those difficult places. As I have learned through my journey, I hope you take away from reading this book, the following messages:

1. Know your strengths and weaknesses. Nobody is perfect. And that's okay. There's no formula to follow, but there are ways you can grow every day. In order to grow, it is important to first know and evaluate how you are doing.

2. Listen and learn. We grow when we are open to learning from those around us. This includes both the good and bad. Anger is never a healthy behavior because pain always finds a way to express itself in surprising, unwelcome ways. Rather, talk through those hard times with honesty and learn from it.

3. **See difficulty as a time of growth and refinement.** Some of the pain and disappointment in our lives is a result of our own choices and actions. Regardless of whether the nasty consequences we suffer are self-inflicted or not, it is amazing how we can bounce back from a setback if we only use that circumstance to help us grow. As someone who has failed many times over, I continue to be amazed by the power of a setback being a setup for a greater comeback. Just as the sun will shine and the rain will fall, it is inevitable that we will face disappointment, pain and difficulty in life. Today, my goal is not so much to be spared from any difficulty as this is unrealistic, but that I can learn from it and use it as a stepping stone for higher heights.

GROW

In

Difficult Places

Learning to See Beauty Beyond the Dark

CHAPTER ONE

Start with Why

I recently had lunch with a colleague and after a wonderful hour of making small talk, my friend complained of how despite their advanced education and credentials, he had not been able to achieve success in his career as compared to another colleague who was not as educated as he was. My friend operated from the assumption that the most educated individual should get the top spot and so could not understand when things didn't go as they assumed, or when others are able to achieve things that defied all assumptions. This led me to reflecting on why some individuals and organizations are more successful than others. What is different in these people that others do not have? Why did Martin Luther King, Jr. led the Civil Rights Movement? He wasn't the only man who suffered in pre-civil rights America and he certainly wasn't the only great orator of the day. Why him? Why is it that the Wright brothers were able to figure out control powered manned flight when there were certainly other teams who were better qualified and funded, and they didn't achieve powered manned flight. The Wright brothers beat them to it. There's something else at play here.

All great and inspiring leaders and organizations in the world, whether it's Apple or Martin Luther King, Jr. or the Wright brothers – they all think, act, and communicate the exact same way and it's the complete opposite to everyone else. They begin with the end in mind; they have a purpose and are driven by that purpose. Every single person and organization in the planet know what they do. Some know how they do it. But very few people and organizations know why they do what they do. And by why I don't mean to make a profit – that's a result. By why I mean, what's your purpose? What's your cause? What's your belief? Why does your organization exist? Successful leaders and organizations, regardless of their size or industry, all think, act, and communicate from the inside out. The example of Apple can help illustrate this point. If Apple were like everyone else, a marketing message from them may sound like this: We make great computers. They are beautifully designed, simple to use, and user friendly. Want to buy one?

That's how most of us communicate. That's how most marketing and sales are done and that's how most of us communicate interpersonally. We say what we do, we say how we are different or how we are better, and we expect some sort of behavior – a purchase or vote or something like that. "Here's our new law firm. We have the best lawyers with the biggest clients. We always perform for our clients – do business with us." "Here's our new car – it gets great gas mileage; it has leather seats – buy our car." But this is uninspiring. Here's how Apple actually communicates – Everything we do we believe in challenging the status quo, we believe in thinking differently. The way we challenge the status quo is by making our products beautifully designed, simple to use, and user friendly. We just happen to make great computers. Want to buy one? Totally different, right? You're ready to buy a computer from me. All I did was reverse the order of the information. People don't buy what you do, people buy why you do it. This explains why some people are perfectly comfortable buying a computer from Apple. Some are also perfectly comfortable buying an MP3 player from Apple, or a phone from Apple or a DVR from Apple. As I said before, Apple is just a computer company. There's nothing that distinguishes them structurally from any of their competitors. Their competitors are all equally qualified to make all of these products.

As leaders, our goal should not be to do business with everybody who needs what you have, rather our goal should be to do business with people who believe what we believe. The goal is not just to hire people who need a job, it is to hire people who believe what you believe. I always say that if you hire people just because they can do a job, they will work for your money. If you hire people who believe what you believe, they will work for you with blood, sweat, and tears. And nowhere else is there a better example of this than with the Wright brothers.

Most people don't know about Samuel Pierpont Langley and back in the early 20th century, the pursuit of powered manned flight was like the dot com of the day. Everybody was trying it. Samuel Pierpont Langley had what we assume to be the recipe for success. Samuel Pierpont Langley was given $50,000 by the War Department to figure out this flying machine. Money was no problem. He held a seat at Harvard and worked at the Smithsonian and was extremely well connected. He knew all the big minds of the day. He hired the best minds money could find and the market conditions were fantastic. The New York Times followed him around everywhere and everyone was rooting for Langley. Then how come we have never heard of Samuel Pierpont Langley? A few hundred miles away in Dayton, Ohio lived Orville and Wilbur Wright. They had none of what we consider to be the recipe for success. They had no money. They paid for their dream with the proceeds from their bicycle shop. Not a single person on the Wright brothers' team had a college education. Not even Orville or Wilbur. The New York Times followed them around nowhere. The difference was that Orville and Wilbur were driven by a cause, a purpose, a belief. They believed that if they could figure out this flying machine, it will change the course of the world. Samuel Pierpont Langley was different. He wanted to be rich and famous. He was in pursuit of the result and riches. Lo and behold look what happened. The people who believed in the Wright brothers' dream worked with them with blood, sweat, and tears. The others just worked for the pay check. They tell stories about how every time the Wright brothers went out, they would have to take five sets of parts because that's how many times they would crash before they came in for supper. And eventually on December 17, 1903, the Wright brothers took flight and no one was there to even experience it. Further proof that Langley was motivated by the wrong thing – the day the Wright brothers took flight, he quit. He could have said, "That's an amazing discovery guys and I will improve upon your technology," but he didn't. He wasn't first, didn't get rich, nor did he get famous, so he quit. People don't buy what you do, they buy why you do it. If you talk about what you believe, you will attract those who believe what you believe.

So why is it important to attract those who believe what you believe? Something called the law of diffusion of innovation. The first two and half percent of our population are our innovators. The next 13.5 percent of our population are our early adopters, the next 34% are your early majority, the late majority, and your laggards. The only reason these people buy touchtone phones is because you can't buy rotary phones anymore. We all sit at various places at various times on this scale but what the law of diffusion of innovation tells us is that if you want mass market success or mass market acceptance of an idea, you cannot have it until you achieve this tipping point between 15 and 18 percent market penetration and then the system tips.

The early majority will not try something until someone else has tried it first. They are more comfortable making those intuitive decisions that are driven by what they believe about the world and not just what product is available. These are the people who stood in line for six hours to buy an iPhone when they first came out. When you could have just walked into a store the next week and bought one off the shelf. These are the people who spent $40,000 on flat screen TVs when they first came out even though the technology was substandard. By the way, they didn't do it because the technology was so great. They did it for themselves, it's because they wanted to be first. People don't buy what you do, they buy why you do it and what you do simply proves what you believe. In fact, people will do the things that prove what they believe. The reason the person bought the iPhone in the first six hours was because of what they believed about the world and how they wanted everybody to see them. They were first.

In the summer of 1963, 250,000 people showed up at the Mall of Washington, DC. to hear Dr. King speak. They sent out no invitations and there was no website to check the date. How do you do that? Well, Dr. King wasn't the only man in America who was a great orator. He wasn't the only man in America who suffered in pre-civil rights America. In fact, some of his ideas were bad but he had a gift. He didn't go around telling people what needed to change in America. He went around and told people what he believed. "I believe, I believe, I believe," he told people. People who believed what he believed took his cause and made it their own and they told people. Some of those people created structures to get the word out to even more people. Lo and behold, 250,000 people showed up on the right day, at the right time to hear him speak. How many of them showed up for him? Zero. They showed up for themselves. It's what they believed about America that got them to travel in a bus for eight hours to stand in the sun in Washington in the middle of August. It wasn't about black versus white. Twenty five percent of the audience was white. Dr. King believed that there were two types of laws in this world: those that are made by a higher authority and those that are made by man and not until all the laws that are made by man are consistent with the laws that are made by a higher authority will we live in a just world. It just so happens that the Civil Rights Movement was the perfect thing to help him bring his cause to life. We follow him not for him, but for ourselves. By the way, he gave the I Have a Dream speech not the I Have a Plan speech. Listen to politicians now with their comprehensive 12-point plans, they don't inspire anybody. There are leaders and then there are those who lead. Leaders hold a position of power or authority but those who lead inspire us, whether they are individuals or organizations, we follow those who lead not because we have to but because we want to. We follow those who lead, not for them but for ourselves. It's those who start with "why", that can inspire those around them or find others who inspire them.

CHAPTER TWO

The Mask That We Wear

Every day in the news we hear stories about people who seem relatively happy with their lives and yet they go and do something horrific, like crash a plane filled with passengers. What the news is revealing is that the man's life was falling apart: a lover had recently left him, his eyesight was becoming such a problem that he was going to have to give up his job and doing the thing he loved most (flying), and he had a history of battling depression.

He wore a mask of the happy man who had it all: a fabulous career and a great relationship. So, when those things fell apart, the only thing he had left to expose to the world was his true self and apparently, he didn't feel that self was worthy of life. Perhaps if he had loved himself more, he would realize that there was more to him than a beautiful girlfriend and a glamorous job.

Why would someone do something so terrible? Depression? A sense of hopelessness? No one really knows, but here is what I know and believe to be true: we all wear masks. We all have to 1) realize that no one is as perfect as we imagine they are, in fact if they are "perfect" then they are probably wearing a mask, so we cannot compare ourselves to them and 2) we should learn to practice self-acceptance, loving ourselves, our true selves, so we don't need to wear a mask because we feel comfortable and at peace with who we are.

I am often taken aback when someone says to me, "You wrote a book about bouncing back so you can't have a bad day!" Really? So, I guess that means all the people who ever wrote books about happiness and self-love never doubt who they are. I am here to share that we all have some issue we are facing every day, whether we write books about it or not. We are all going through something. No one gets off easy!

Be honest with yourself. Recognize when, maybe during stressful times or when faced with negative situations, you are tempted to don a mask instead of loving yourself and asking for help if necessary. When we present our authentic selves, loved ones are more comfortable trusting us and reaching out for help when needed.

We all wear masks from time to time: in our words, our habits, and our practices. We have an arsenal of crutches and shortcuts that slowly but surely hide who we are. They are things that prop us up and help us hide. We hide from our feelings and our desires. We hide from who we might become. We drink coffee as a mask for how tired we are, or to replace what is really a lack of motivation for a certain project we're involved in. It masks how tired you are of caring for a newborn infant, or how miserable your boss's cutting remarks make you. The alcohol that you drink at night masks the fear and the stress you feel from not having control during your day. Perhaps it helps to cover up the loneliness of your cubicle or help you get through another night. We project false smiles of protection to hide our fears, and to be desirable. We wear high heels and new clothes and carry certain bags and advertisements to show a sense of self, a projection, an idea. We use extroversion to be well liked. We chase busy to mask our fear of not leaving an impact. We cover a lot of things up.

Scars we carry, stories we hold, work we're afraid of doing.

It's not always bad to have a mask, but they can't be our only way of dealing with the world. If we spend the entire time warding off the world and hiding from ourselves, we'll miss the best parts. By hiding from the world, we hide ourselves, and we lose a piece of our souls. Many of us have lost touch with ourselves, our souls, with the tender, tired, scared part of itself. Here's the catch. Releasing our mask requires *feeling*. It requires having a real, honest, scary, less-than-desirable *feeling*. Letting go of your mask means you might need to say, "*I'm tired. No, I don't want to do this or I'm scared. I'm scared of messing up. I'm scared of doing a bad job. I'm worried that I won't be liked. I'm worried that I might try, and I won't be good at it.*"

Letting the barrier down requires guts and honesty with ourselves.

Our feelings are clues. Feelings are way points in an uncertain world, direction markers that guide us back into the brilliance of ourselves, if we'll allow it. The trouble is it can be uncomfortable and downright painful. Feelings you haven't had in years might surface to remind you of areas of internal work you still have to do.

Masks are protection too. Sometimes pulling down the mask and showing your face requires gentleness and slowness. Your mask might have served you at some point. A therapist reminded me that these coping mechanisms shouldn't always be disarmed quickly. Children of abuse who learned how to harden and deaden their senses build masks in order to survive those times. These mechanisms and masks were useful--they help us survive. They got you there. They protected. Unlocking them too quickly without new ways of being can also be damaging.

We also need to show different faces to the world at different times to adapt to our roles and situations. Everyone changes his or her behaviors to meet challenges and circumstances. We have all had to bite our tongue, or wear clothes that are not totally comfortable, to make a certain impression. Our words and actions may not always be our first choice.

The interesting truth is that we present ourselves differently to different people. The way you act with your mother is usually not exactly the same way you act with friends or your boss. The language you use, way you dress, topics you discuss, and your actions all change as you play your roles.

It can be fun, as well as necessary at times, to play with masks and disguises. We all do this. Each of us can be on our "best behaviour" (whatever that might look like) and play a role to adapt and cope in this complex, ever changing world. **It's important to learn what to do and say to fit in.** I'm sure everyone can give examples of how they learned to avoid certain behaviors and topics in specific situations. These adaptations are important if we want to interact successfully with a variety of people.

But you don't want to confuse your adaptations with the "true you". You may be a parent, child, sibling, employee, boss, friend, neighbor, lover, colleague, contributor, or competitor. Each persona, in various situations, may require different words and actions.

When I teach my students, it is useful for me to match the language and demeanor of an instructor to create rapport and facilitate learning. My intent is to help my class learn and grow. Is this genuine? I believe it is; yet my choice of words and my actions may be modified from how I naturally prefer to speak and act. This is an adaptation.

The key is to find the purpose behind the adaptation. What are the threads that tie together your changing words and actions? For example, you may be at your best when you are focused on the moment, playing with ideas and possibilities, searching for reasons and explanations, connecting with others, knowing everything is going according to plan, or being flexible and spontaneous. These threads may show up across your adaptive behaviors. By clarifying your motivations and interests across all of your roles, you'll discover your core sense of purpose and enjoyment. This is the "authentic you" that, will be empowering and gratifying.

It's not always bad to have a mask, but they can't be our only way of dealing with the world.

CHAPTER THREE

Living in the Learning Zone

I walked into my office today to find one of my colleagues and friend standing with a gift-wrapped box for me. When I opened it, it was a big brass bucket with my initials engraved on the front and filled with 20 or so small gifts. The following narrative recounts what led to this day.

Things had not been going well for my friend. He was in a slump. He was working harder but going nowhere. He barely saw his kids, his marriage was suffering and his health was not the best. He was struggling in every part of his life. At work, business was slow and the pressure to improve was "unbearable". He was ready to give up because his doubts about his leadership abilities were overwhelming the confidence he once had. He needed to talk to someone who would listen and offer suggestions without judging him. His life was careening out of control and something needed to change. He knew he had to reach out to someone. He chose to call me and this began a series of weekly conversations between us that would span over 12 weeks. The following is an account of one of our sessions that I would like to share:

Have you seen the movie *Ground Hog Day?* I asked my friend. The one where Bill Murray lives the same day over and over and over again? Yes, he responded. Well, that's the same way a lot of people live their lives. They wake up and do the same thing over and over and over again because that's where they are comfortable - until it's time to retire. A forceful enemy to our potential is our comfort zone. When my friend first approached me, without knowing it, he described what it was to be like in the comfort zone. And when things changed for him at his job, he was no longer comfortable and didn't know what to do or where to go. For any of us to be our best, we cannot allow ourselves to become complacent in our comfort zone. We need to be reaching for improvement. To fulfill our potential, we need to move out of our comfort zone and into the "learning zone". Let me explain what the "learning zone" is.

There are three rooms in the "learning zone". The first room is the reading room. Over the years, I have collected more than 500 books on healthcare and leadership from the many courses I have taken either as a student or have taught as an educator. The value I offer to my students now, is the wisdom of all the talented people who have written these books. You see, we learn more by reading more. I'm living proof that the more you learn, the more you earn. I read one study which found that most people do not read one non-fiction book in a year. You would think books are scarce or expensive. There is an abundance of books at every public library for free. From my experience the question is not whether we have the time or money, the question is do we have the discipline to set aside time every day to read. When we make it a priority to read, our knowledge will likely make us the obvious choice for promotion when the next job opening at a higher position comes up as we would be better prepared to assume that role.

The second room in the learning zone is the listening room. Another study I read found that the principle reason top executives fail was arrogance, out of control egos, and insensitivity. When we forget to listen, we become insensitive to the needs and desires of the individuals on our team. Arrogance, out-of-control egos and insensitivity are part of the management trap - a danger zone that we should all try very much to avoid. Anytime we gather new information, it helps us make better decisions. I have learned to listen better by making better use of my time. The average person spends over 500 hours per year in their car. For me, I spend most of that time listening to a motivational or inspirational tape and it has greatly influenced me.

The third room in the learning zone is the giving room. I truly believe that as leaders we cannot succeed without giving back. Hearses don't have luggage racks for a reason; our legacy is what we leave others. As an early careerist, one of the requirements my own mentor had me commit to was to teach others what he would be teaching me. My mentor's purpose in making this a requirement was so that I would become more accountable. The more we teach, the more accountable we become to what we're teaching.

And while we all agree that we need to become life-long learners, the truth of the matter is that nothing is going to change unless we make specific goals for improvement. I am reminded of the story of people who went to the airport to wait for their ship to come in. The only problem is, ships don't go to airports and so, it is with us too. If we want our ship to come in, we have to go to where the ships are. In personal improvement, the ships are in goals - specific, measurable, and obtainable goals. I've found that goals can become the strongest force for self-motivation - they are the track to run the course. Yet less than five percent of all people set specific goals. In my opinion, there are four main reasons why people fail to set goals.

First, is that they don't know the importance of goal

setting. Every great accomplishment I know about has begun with a goal written down on a sheet of paper. Achieving the goal is automatic, setting the goal is the issue. Second, most people don't know how to set goals. At each point of my journey, I write down specific actions I will take to be successful. I do this because writing clarifies the goal and commits me to it. Third, is that sometimes people are afraid of failure. If you have no goals, you're not risking failure. I think we should be the exact opposite - (fail faster, and more often). Failure is a prelude to success. To become successful, we have to fail more and often. We need to set goals that help us become more successful even if we fail to accomplish the goal. Fourth, goals require people to leave their comfort zone. That can be scary for many people because it often involves having to learn new skills. Over the years, I have learned that most people do not want to follow someone who loses their health or family because they work all the time. People want to follow others who are balanced in all areas, not just work. So, for me, I have watched and learned from others who are fantastic goal setters and goal achievers. Leaders who have balance in their life.

Finally, we need to stay positive. Of course, we will become discouraged somewhere along the way, but we don't need to give up. The world is not full of Pollyannas. Bad things do happen even to the best people. Golf is a great teacher of life's lessons as well as leadership lesson. I've learned that in every round of golf, three bad things are going to happen that are not deserved. You may hit the ball in the middle of the fairway only to discover the ball in an old divot. Or, you hit the perfect shot right before the wind gusts, and your shot lands just short, buried in the bunker. Or perhaps your prefect putt moves off course because someone didn't take time to fix their ball mark. In similar fashion, unfair things happen in life and in business. The question then should not be "Are unfair things going to happen?", but rather the question should be "How are you going to react to whatever happens?"

One of the greatest individuals in my opinion, I consider the wisest and most positive person I know, did not have much money or formal education. Yet to me she earned a PhD in common sense. One of the nuggets of wisdom from this friend that I will always remember is how to face problems and be positive, no matter the situation. She used to tell the story of how everyone could go to a field and line up around the perimeter. While standing on the edge of the field, each person is given the opportunity to throw their problem into the middle of the field. Once all of the problems have been thrown in, you have your choice of which ones to pick up and take home. Most people will probably pick up their own problem and go back home, realizing that they really didn't have it bad after all. I think she is right on the money with her story. So much of life is about attitude and how we handle what life throws our way. Life is good - even when a situation appears to be the worst. Stay positive and help make another's life better.

It took courage for my friend to call me several weeks ago. He would not have called unless he was at a point where he had nothing to lose, but he still had the courage to call. I understand that feeling of being at the end of one's rope. I've been there before and also had made a similar call to my own mentor. If my friend hadn't made the call, nothing most likely would have changed except he would probably be even more frustrated. So, as we enter into a new year, let me ask you: What are you going to do differently? At the risk of sounding corny, the big brass bucket of gifts my friend gave me represents what I had done during the past weeks of listening and sharing with him. With a lump forming in my throat, my friend told me that I had filled his bucket with the gifts of insight and wisdom. And as we said farewell wishing each other a wonderful holiday, I reminded him of the commitment that I made him take when we first began our sessions - to teach others what I had taught him. I thanked him for the bucket of gifts, took a deep breath and felt very honored that he had called on me and allowed me to work with him.

CHAPTER FOUR

The Joy of Rejection

This week I received a rejection letter for a highly coveted membership into a professional organization. As an individual who has worked hard all my academic and professional career, and achieved outstanding accomplishments, this came as a big surprise to me as I have never experienced an outright rejection of any kind before. This rejection was a big bruise to my ego, and confidence and initially led me to a path of depression for what I "considered" as having lost. It was during this period of deep reflection that the following realization came to me which I want to share; rejection is a blessing in disguise, it is a gift to be celebrated and learned from.

I realized that there is a big difference between what rejection is and is not. Rejection is not a "you are not good enough", it is a "you are not the right fit". A square peg does not fit into a round hole not because it is "not good enough" but because it is "not the right shape". I recall a position I interviewed for several years ago and never got a call back and how disappointed I was for not making the shortlist. Looking back now, I realize how unprepared I was at that time for the position. In retrospect, I am glad I never got the position.

What a blessing it is when we can see ourselves the way other people see us. Others can easily identify characteristics in us that we do not see in ourselves or tend to ignore. So, when we get rejected, it is another way of saying this is not a fit. What they did was merely to highlight a dissonance before we realize or acknowledge it ourselves. As humans, it is our nature to fall for the excitement of being sought-after over subtle but important considerations such as whether or not a connection is the right fit. This becomes even more important when the opportunity or position comes with increase prestige, wealth, or fame. This certainly was the case in my situation. Membership in this organization brings with it professional prestige and increased visibility.

I also come to the realization that when rejected, we should learn to move on and not allow it to define who and what we are (or aren't). The problem with me (and many of us) as I came to realize is that our need for feeling validated takes a greater hold and influences how we think of ourselves. Social validation is like sugar to a dieter, a quick and often short-lived fix.

In retrospect, I realize that the hurt I experienced from being rejected had to do more with my need for self-aggrandizement more than the anything else. I regret the many instances I have pursue opportunities purely for self-centered reasons rather than seek to find the right path for me. So rather than spend any more time feeling sorry for myself and being depressed due to the rejection letter, I have decided to focus on pursuing opportunities that improve my abilities leading to more fruitful results besides my ego. I have decided to focus my emotions and time into building my existing strengths and exploring areas for improvement. Without this realization, I would spend a lifetime pursuing unfulfilled goals and dreams; living a life without purpose.

When you focus on your purpose, you can soar in whatever you do and our passion for what we do will not dissipate when we face rejection; it will only increase. That is why rejection is a blessing. It's a clear sign that an opportunity was not right for us. It's to be welcomed because the reality is that if the other side is not 100% excited, they are not right.

Today, in my office, hangs a framed picture of the rejection letter. One of my graduate students walked in and after reading the letter, asked me how I could stand framing it and displaying it so boldly which is an acknowledgement of my failure. She explained that from a young age she had always been taught to set goals and achieve whatever she desired and my display of the rejection letter, makes her confused. My response to her was that, it was a blessing in disguise to me. Reminding myself of that letter is what drives me to give my best in any and all that I do. I reminded her that rejection is not failure. Sooner or later we all experience rejection (if you haven't, bet me, you soon will). Failure is when we give up. It is how we handle rejection that determines where we'll end up.

When you focus on your purpose, you can soar in whatever you do.

CHAPTER FIVE

Knowing Yourself is the Beginning of all wisdom.

~ Aristotle

Back when I was a child, I used to get called naïve at least once a week. Now, as an adult, I continue to hear the same comment a million times from friends, family and acquaintances. People would tell me: "You have a great personality, but you're pretty naïve." For many years, I've taken this to heart, and in a pretty negative way, thinking there was something wrong with me. I've tried to "suck it up" and toughen up in hopes that I'd finally achieve this badass trait everyone keeps telling me to acquire. Today, I'm glad I can finally shut down the critics and be true to myself. As a young careerist, I took off on my own and took the risk of going without guaranteed income. I tied my financial fortunes to my own efforts, rather than to the wisdom of senior executives. And it's worked out well so far. But I'm working on something bigger these days, and I want to revisit some of my naive ideas from my younger days. Because I still believe that being NAIVE is one of the best ways to become great.

When I began my career over a decade ago, I quickly realized that there are certain circumstances out of my control. I was courageous enough to recognize that while something such as the weather was outside of my sphere of influence, there are things I could change. It is important that we know the difference between what we can control and what we cannot as we go about our days. For example, we can control what time we leave the house, but we cannot control traffic. So, we can leave the house about half an hour earlier than it takes to get to work to account for terrible traffic. There is nothing wrong with being naïve, as we are all inexperience in way one or another at some point, but it is wrong if we do not recognize we are being naïve. The most intelligent people I know are not the ones who act like they know everything. They are the ones who recognize they do not know most things, and that they are always ready and willing to change, adapt, and learn something new. Everyone has something to teach someone, but only the wise realize that they can learn from everyone.

One of my favorite quotes also happens to be synonymous with Alcoholics Anonymous meetings. The quote come from the Serenity Prayer by Reinhold Niebuhr, and begins as such: *"God grant me the serenity to accept the things I cannot change; Courage to change the things I can; wisdom to know the difference"*.

I find that this quote can easily apply to our everyday lives, and specifically how we approach choices in our careers. As we begin our careers, we lack wisdom due to our lack of experience.

We begin our careers with a passionate albeit emblazoned naivety. This allows us to appear approachable, attracting mentors who see us as driven, but in need of someone who can show us the way to a more professional and experienced path. As we get older, this naivety becomes less cute and more aggravating. The seasoned professional's naivety swiftly underscores what remains of their professional prowess. In many ways, I certainly was naïve. But sometimes it's good to be naive even if it makes you suffer in the beginning. The essence is not to lose this naivety but to educate it. A certain amount of innocence is beneficial, but you still have to adapt."

As I see it, the two biggest enemies to naivety is university and getting older. Right now, I'm in the process of both. I want to share my enthusiasm, before it is reduced to an analysis, from an older critical me, of a younger naive me. **This tribute to naivety is more than anything** a reminder to me. A reminder so when many years later, I find myself wiser and brighter, — with the ability to spot a mistake in an idea, I will have this manifest, written by a younger unsophisticated version of myself to remind me that being naive, open-minded, optimistic and trustful beyond reason can be a good thing.

I recently enrolled in a philosophy course at a local university. Now, I look back at some amazing lectures with the most brilliant and engaged teachers I have ever spent time with. A mind opening experience in so many ways. Especially, the end of one lecture keeps coming back to me. One professor, whom everyone including me admired, looked at us in the end of a lecture, smiled and said: "Philosophy is to look critical at everything." In life as in this class, whether we like it or not, we take a critical view at too much critical thinking. In the human brain age, which is dominated by reason — I truly believe naivety can be a good thing. As I look forward to a life with education and philosophy in abundance, I feel a need to remind myself about the enormous strength of the naive, intuitive and imaginative mind. A need to celebrate the naive heroes who accomplished great stuff. **The list of heroes is long** — think of personalities like Steve Jobs, Einstein, Gandhi, Goethe and Jonathan Livingston. It seems to me that many great things came from people who had a naive mindset in some form.

Naivety is often mentioned as a bad thing — by politicians when they attack each other. By journalist, analyst and academics when they express their opinion on something. And by so called experts — who use their magical calculator as an argument to kill even the best and most ambitious naive vision. **I acknowledge that having reliable politicians and executives is more than a good thing.** It's necessary. The same goes for critical thinking — I do not even dare to think where we would be without it. But I think it is unfair how naivety is taken hostage, as something that is always bad. Naivety is a beautiful and rare gift — present in every child and few adults. For me, and the dictionaries, naivety is synonymous with being unsophisticated, lacking knowledge, being natural, intuitive, trustful, instinctive, open-minded, and imaginative. It follows, that such a mindset will get everyone in trouble at some point. It will fill your heart with love, betray you, take you down endless dead ends and waste your time repeatedly. I have had countless disappointments in life already — because of naivety. Yes, naivety can be our best friend and our worst enemy. I do not think we can control it, but maybe we can understand it. Perhaps we should just accept that naivety enriches our life in unpredictable ways — for good and for bad. Our desire to avoid disappointment is dangerous, since that always involve a certain mistrust to naivety.

We are in a constant race to produce more. Population growth and demands are booming. At the same time, we have endangered nature's resources and ecosystems like never before. Visions about the future, and I mean incredibly radical visions, is needed more than ever. As soon as there is a creative naive vision — humans have the potential to, in a magical way, rise above ordinary limits. We have done it so many times. I get excited about improbable ideas.

Naivety continues to be misunderstood. It's a good thing. It's a part of the solution — not something we should avoid at all costs. It's the bridge to optimism, trust, radical new inventions, creative ideas and a sustainable world. Never blame a person for being naive, by suggesting something you find too ambitious, too optimistic or just impossible. Blame those, who do not have the courage to be imaginative and explore the impossible.

Traditional think tanks and too many experts in politics, newspapers and companies are focusing on the possible incremental improvements. Their only weapon to understand the potential of an idea, is a calculator, an analysis of the past and an estimate of the future. That is not only extremely boring. It also prevents us from breakthroughs and creativity in science, society, business etc. How far do we need to go back in time, before landing on the moon was impossible? The internet — impossible? Smartphones — impossible? In the clear light of history — naivety turns out to be a great strategy, if you want to say something about the future. Not knowing what you're doing and not knowing what you "should" know and being just a little bit dumb or naïve is sometimes a good thing. Knowing too much can be a bad thing. Whether it's in sports, business, or whatever, knowledge often limits what you do. The examples are many: Entrepreneurs who jump in and make new ventures work despite many people with much more knowledge and experience saying it won't work. Athletes who accomplish things because they didn't know they shouldn't be able to. Scientists not listening to what others have said and coming up with breakthroughs.

I love coaching young students. Why? Because they don't know what they can't do; they think they can do anything. And so often, they can. They do things that others with more experience would say can't or should not be done. They succeed for one reason: They go for it. I know a salesperson who doesn't always do things "by the book," but he makes things happen. That's because he isn't limited by what others think. I'm not saying he's dumb. In fact, he's very smart, but he doesn't let the rules or what others think is the right way, get in the way of getting things done.

So, how do you use what you know without that knowledge getting in the way? Without it limiting you? The trick, of course, is knowing when to trust your knowledge and experience, and when to turn your brain off and just go for it. Try it. Turn off your brain; stop thinking about what can and can't be done; stop thinking about what the "right" way is to do or think about something; stop listening to people that say you can't do that… and just do it. Try it for a while. The problem is that you – and most everyone else – have been programmed to think in a certain way. So, until you consciously change the way you think, you'll keep thinking the way you've always thought. Consciously and deliberately act naïve.

At this age, I want to keep and cultivate my naivety, trust and openness. I want to keep the remaining of my childish mind for as long as possible. Of course, it is possible to have both! But how can we learn to devise bold and innovative hypothesis? I can assure you it is not a part of the university curriculum. My current favorite business role model is Richard Branson. Usually styled these days as "uber-successful billionaire, Sir Richard Branson." Branson spent much of his business life doing things that were entirely clueless:

- His decision (while still at school at 15 years old) to launch a national magazine instead of focusing on his studies was clueless.
- His decision to start a record store when he knew nothing about retail was clueless. This was followed by clueless decisions to build a recording studio, a record label, and then international divisions of Virgin Records. Utterly clueless, everyone.
- His decision to start an airline, a tremendously complex and risky business that he knew absolutely nothing about, was impressively clueless.
- His penchant for launching businesses just because the names make him smile (Virgin Bride, Virgin Snow) is clueless.
- His diversification of the Virgin brand to more than 360 companies, without a clear connecting thread

like Procter & Gamble or Coke have, is often called clueless.

- His decision to create the world's first "space line" (an airline for outer space) wasn't just clueless, it was downright loony.

Branson is my favorite kind of naive businessman. The kind who tries everything that sounds like it would be fun, works like crazy to make it happen, and knows when to walk away from decisions that don't work out. Today, of course, he's widely lionized. But for decades, he was generally considered to be an entertaining, naive flake. He's currently worth close to $4 billion. Give or take a million or two.

Having a clue is vastly overrated. I am not a big fan of the expression "Leap and the net will appear." More often, it works out to "Leap and the floor will appear." Naiveté is about rejecting stupid definitions of maturity. It's about brushing aside rules that no longer make any sense (if they ever did). Naiveté is about seeing a bigger picture. About being brave enough to ignore conventional advice that doesn't apply to you, doesn't make you happy, and may not even make you any money. Naiveté is not willful ignorance. It makes plenty of room for curiosity and learning. It makes lots of room for experimentation and thoughtful observation. But it has no patience for ruthlessness (except with ourselves), jockeying for status, or **trashing your conscience** in the name of a paper success. Don't ignore the facts, especially the ugly ones. But do understand that it's your game. You get to write the rules.

When I first began writing, I wasn't focused crafting the next Great American Novel. Instead, I said to myself, "I'll bet I can write something that's AT LEAST as good as the stuff I read." **If I had done my research first—uncovering what it would take to "break in" to publishing,** I WOULD HAVE QUIT BEFORE I STARTED. If you let the fear of the unknown stop you from even starting, you won't start.

So, choose instead to be naïve. Focus on a personal, fulfilling goal of shaping your dreams. "Successful" people often have one thing in common: **They refuse to maintain the status quo, adhere to the world's rules, or follow the norm.** If you will allow yourself to "be naïve" and NOT let the huge world of expectations get to you, opportunities will arise. Your initial efforts probably won't be the pinnacle of achievement—but they're COMPLETE. That should be your goal. You'll learn more going through the processes than you ever will in a school.

But you may ask **"what if I fail?".** If you define an achievable and responsible goal, and fail while reaching for it, you've most likely gotten way ahead of the competition already. Our **fear of failure** leads us toward procrastination, lack of motivation, and, well, failure. But by being naïve and reaching for the most out-of-reach goals and successes we'll at least be motivated by the fact that we're part of the few who can say we've tried it. So, let's get specific: what things are you reaching for? In what ways have you succeeded (or failed miserably) and in what ways can you be more naïve?

Everyone has something to teach someone, but only the wise realize that they can learn from everyone.

CHAPTER SIX

Finding Strength in Being Vulnerable

At a professional conference where I spoke a few months ago, I shared with the audience many of the challenges and hardship I had faced along my professional career, from failing exams, being fired, unemployed, to dealing with depression. At the end of the session, one of the attendees walked up to me in amazement to express her astonishment at the fact that I was so brave to share my failures in such an open way. She said "I know vulnerability is a good way to be, but I find it difficult. The moment I notice that feel I have lost control of a situation, rather than keep feeling vulnerable, I move away from it. For example, when I am with people, rather than discuss my feelings, admitting my imperfections, or letting my faults show themselves, I am more often concerned with looking as perfect as I can be and engage in more superficial conversations." This interaction leads me to think about the question "Why does vulnerability feel so scary and awkward sometimes?" "Is vulnerability the same as weakness?" In our culture, we associate vulnerability with emotions we want to avoid such as fear, shame, and uncertainty. **Merriam-Webster defines vulnerability as**

"easily hurt or harmed physically, mentally, or emotionally: open to attack, harm, or damage: To many of us, vulnerability is a scary word.

Most of us can relate to times when we expressed an emotion and it was not received well, so we develop suppression techniques. In the case of the audience member who approached me, she stated that her parents expected her to have her stuff together and be a good example because she is the eldest child. Emotion was looked down upon, and keeping it together was rewarded. In my humble opinion, I think some of us have lost sight of the fact that vulnerability is also the birthplace of joy, belonging, creativity, authenticity, and love. It is something that we should learn and practice. Why should we practice something that so clearly opens us to hurt, harm, or damage? Surely, this can't be right.

Well, as it turns out, when we learn to become open, honest, and yes – vulnerable to others (and ourselves), we open the door for deeper connections. We become the person who steps out into the unknown, risking ourselves for a cause that stirs our souls. We say, "I LOVE YOU," first without knowing what will happen. We take risks because we deeply feel that it is the right thing to do. When we are brutally honest with ourselves, we can embrace our strengths with the understanding that we are not super-human, but we do have value and a contribution to make in this world. As the famous author Stephen Russell puts it, "Vulnerability is the only authentic state. Being vulnerable means being open, for wounding, but also for pleasure. Being open to the wounds of life means also being open to the bounty and beauty. Don't mask or deny your vulnerability: it is your greatest asset. Be vulnerable: quake and shake in your boots with it. The new goodness that is coming to you, in the form of people, situations, and things can only come to you when you are vulnerable, i.e. open."

Although it may seem like we are protecting ourselves, suppressing our expression erects walls around our hearts and reinforces beliefs about it not being safe to share our genuine feelings with another. As a result, we form relationships that are based more on fear than love. Rather than being truly authentic with others, we become strategic. Vulnerability is discounted because it just feels too risky. We cannot truly experience the delicious emotions that a human relationship offers if we are not authentic. Please do not underestimate the healing power of vulnerability. Don't let fear stop you when it comes to being raw and real with others. To fully feel the love and connection we all yearn for, vulnerability is required. Think of someone you feel very close to. There have been times when you have shared a feeling with that person that felt risky to expose, yet when it was received with love, rather than judgment, your relationship got stronger. Vulnerability connects us. It is a great gift we give to another person when we let them see behind any masks or walls of emotional protection. Moreover, vulnerability is a priceless gift to give to ourselves.

If you crave authentic and genuine connection, here are some tips for how to be vulnerable:

1. Choose wisely: Begin practicing vulnerability with someone who will not judge you, advise you, or attempt to interrupt your process. This person can be a dear friend, family member, mentor, coach or counselor, who will receive the gift of your vulnerability with compassion.

2. Ask for what you want: Create the context for sharing an authentic conversation by asking if the other person is willing to just listen. You can also request that they do not offer any advice unless you specifically ask for it. The purpose of vulnerability is not about problem solving. It is about exposing and releasing.

3. State what is: If you feel nervous or perhaps even ashamed, I suggest calling it out by stating, "I feel ashamed," or, "I am nervous to share this." Remember the key ingredients of vulnerability are authenticity and intimacy. Let yourself be seen!

4. Share from your heart, not your head: Be aware of not recycling your emotions by just talking about them, judging them or analyzing them. Let yourself cry. Ride waves of anger or frustration by not restraining your voice or editing your words.

5. Shine light on shame: Tell the secrets you have locked away because you've been too ashamed to speak them aloud.

6. Let yourself be messy: Forget about grammar, making sense or looking pretty while you cry. Be free with your expression!

Creating honest and genuine connections requires a willingness to be vulnerable. Only while bringing down our guard are, we able to effectively examine why certain unsavory situations occur repeatedly in our lives. Ironically, this kind of vulnerability requires courage. So be courageous, exercise your vulnerability, and invite love and connection into your life today. It is never too late.

CHAPTER SEVEN

Finding the Elusive Work-Life Balance

In the years following obtaining my doctoral degree, I have spent a great deal of time working too hard, neglecting family to advance my career. Today, as I experience my own version of the proverbial "mid-life crisis", I have decided to turn my life around and address the thorny issues of work-life balance. One of the decisions made as I experience this phase of life is to spend more time with family. So, a couple years ago, I got a job working from home which afforded me the ability to do whatever and whenever I wanted. In the last few years, all I have learned about work-life balance is that it is easy to balance work and life when you don't have to work.

My struggles in the last couple of years with this issue has brought me to the following realizations which I would like to share. The first is that there are certain jobs and careers that are fundamentally incompatible with being meaningfully engaged on a day-to-day basis with a young family. The reality of the society that we're in is that there are millions of people leading lives of quiet, screaming desperation, working long, hard hours at jobs they hate to enable them to buy things they don't need to impress people they don't like, or even know.

The second realization is that the government or a corporation is not going to solve this issue for us. It is up to us as individuals to take control and responsibility for the type of lives that we want to lead. If you don't design your life, someone else will design it for you, and you may just not like their idea of balance. It is important that we never put the quality of our lives in the hands of a corporation. Corporations are inherently designed to get as much out of you [as] they can get away with. It's in their nature; it's in their DNA; it's what they do -- even the good, well-intentioned companies. A previous employer provided childcare facilities in the workplace which was wonderful and enlightened. On the other hand, it was a nightmare because it meant spending more time at the office. We have to be responsible for setting and enforcing the boundaries that we want in our life.

The third realization is that we have to give careful consideration to the time frame that we choose to judge our balance. As I considered transitioning back to working at the office, I made a list of those elements of my life that I cherished which gave quality and meaning to my life. They include: wake up at 9 am, go for a walk, having breakfast while watching the morning news, do 4 hours of work, meet a friend for lunch at the local bar, do another 2 hours of work, go out for happy hour with friends, dinner with family, attend neighborhood association meeting, and bed at 10pm. But we all know this is wishful thinking! Being realistic, I realize one cannot do it all in one day. As such, we have to elongate the time frame upon which we judge the balance in our life so that we do not fall into the trap of "I'll have a life when I retire, when my kids have left home, when my wife has divorced me, or I've got no mates or interests left." After I retire is too long.

The fourth realization is that we need to approach balance in a balanced way. One of my longtime friends and professional colleagues (who shall remain anonymous to protect their privacy) was complaining about how completely out of balance their life was. Their complaints included working 12-14 hours days (which included a 2-hour commute), lack of personal relationships, and no outside interests besides work. Their solution to "sorting life out" was to join a gym. As much as I support and advocate for physical exercise, there are other parts to life -- there's the intellectual side; there's the emotional side; there's the spiritual side. And to be balanced, I believe we have to attend to all of those areas -- not just do 50 stomach crunches.

An incident that happened several months ago led to me gain this new perspective. I had the opportunity to pick up my young nephew from school and spend the day with him while his mother was busy at a business meeting. Being a school age kid, we spent the day at the local park, playing games, went to the local Chuck-E-Cheese for pizza, and back home by 6pm for bath and bedtime. After a long, exhausting and fulfilled day with a 6-year-old, I finally put him to bed and as I said good night walking out to the door, he said, "This has been the best day of my life." It is interesting to note that I hadn't done anything special. Hadn't taken him to Disney World or bought him a PlayStation. And this brings me to my point: it is the small things that matter. Being more balanced doesn't mean dramatic upheaval in your life. With the smallest investment in the right places, you can radically transform the quality of your relationships and the quality of your life. When we do this, we can begin to change society's definition of success away from the moronically simplistic notion that the person with the most money when he dies wins, to a more thoughtful and balanced definition of what a life well lived looks like. And that, I think, is how we achieve the elusive work-life balance.

CHAPTER EIGHT

The Paradox of Success: When Winning at Work Means Losing at Life

"The first and best victory is to conquer self; to be conquered by self is, of all things, the most shameful and vile."
~Plato

Today, I got the sad news that my friend (who for privacy reasons, I will refer to as Mark) took his own life. My friend Mark was a very bright, very talented and very successful man who had everything going for him. A successful career, family, and friends who loved him. Suicide is tragic enough, but it's particularly bewildering when young people who appear to have it all take their own lives. Many people often wonder why people who seem so successful commit such a desperate act when they have everything. Money, fame, fortune, what more could one person want? So, I wanted to share a few thoughts about success, stress and suicide. This is what I refer to as the paradox of success; when winning at work means losing at life. My friend Mark had it all. He crushed high school. Was on the track team, leadership roles, AP classes. He had highly engaged parents who encouraged him often but noticed every potentially slipping grade. He kept the hustle torch burning in college, where he tutored kids, joined a Christian organization, and soon experienced the deflating knowledge that there were other students who were more talented, smarter, more accomplished already. While most of us can remember the precise moment in which we became acquainted with our limitations, we muddle through, accepting this as part of the experience of being alive—there will always be someone prettier, more successful, more talented, more accomplished. It's up to us to carve out some unique identity in the world that means something to us in spite of this truth, which cannot be altered.

For some this realization can be the beginning of a downward spiral from which recovery often seems out of reach. What you and I would call disappointments in life, to them feel like big failures. In retrospect, I now understand how my friend must have felt. He became quite attached early on to academic praise, to hearing his parents brag about his accomplishments. It became a defining aspect of his self-esteem and self-fulfilment. My friend, Mark, was a planner, mapping out his career years in advance at a time when plenty of students might be content to use college to figure things out.

Then there is social media. Friend's lives, as told through selfies, showed them having more fun, making more friends and going to better parties. Even the meals they posted to Instagram looked more delicious. And it's in this chasm between the perception of the lives of others and the seemingly inferior reality of your own that the darkest thoughts can grow. One of the most common misconceptions about suicide is that your life must be pretty bad for you to want to kill yourself. But, crucially, it's really the PERCEIVED DISCREPANCY that matters to the depressed person more than any outside view. An interesting fact is that most people with depression don't kill themselves, so mental health is not the explanation for suicide that so many think it is. Rory O'Connor a recognized expert on suicide identified a trait common to those with suicidal thoughts, social perfectionism. This is about what you believe others expect of you. It is not about what you expect of yourself nor is it anything to do with what others actually think or expect of you. It is about your interpretation of it. This leads people to believe that they have let others down or have failed to be good enough in some way. It is the way that your thoughts and emotions combine to convince you that you are less than perfect, that you are not living up to expectation. For men, combined with the gender stereotype and social demands, these expectations can be around being the breadwinner, providing a good role model for the family, it can be competitive, or achievement focused where people feel they are defined by their success in the workplace, their wealth or power.

Social media is well documented in making most of us feel, at one time or another, that our lives are uniquely shitty when held side by side with the travel, food, and family photos of others—people who've seemingly mastered living in the moment, winning at life. But most of us find a way to quiet those voices or reconcile them: Things are never quite what they appear on the outside, we remind ourselves. Everyone suffers in some way. Young people are at a greater disadvantage. Most simply haven't lived enough to know this intimately, to understand that comparing your life to another is a fool's errand. A friend of mine theorizes that by age 35, most everyone you know has suffered something awful directly or via someone they care about—a parent's death, a miscarriage, cancer, divorce, failed career. It humanizes us.

Most people who kill themselves actually lived better-than-average lives. Suicide rates are higher in nations with higher standards of living than in less prosperous nations; higher in US states with a better quality of life; higher in societies that endorse individual freedoms; higher in areas with better weather; in areas with seasonal change, they are higher during the warmer seasons; and they're higher among college students that have better grades and parents with higher expectations. Such idealistic conditions actually heighten suicide risk because they often create unreasonable standards for personal happiness, thereby rendering people more emotionally fragile in response to unexpected setbacks. So, when things get a bit messy, such people, many of whom appear to have led mostly privileged lives, have a harder time coping with failures.

But it takes a long time to acquire the understanding that all of us are flawed and dealing with our own particular baggage—and that some of us are just better at certain things, including the art of making everything look perfect. So many young people, are trapped in this swirl of hyper-achievement and pressure. But they are missing one critical piece: They simply don't know yet how to fail. They have been so focused on getting it right, winning to set themselves up for a good life, that no one has explained that it's OK to go back to the drawing board and start fresh, to scrap everything and try again. That in some ways, doing that sooner than later is itself a gift.

Connecting your success to your self-worth and then once you are successful you realize your life isn't any better and money amplified your problems. In the past, I got stuck in this. Thinking success would make me feel better and even after six figure income, I still felt like shit and wanted more. It is important to find joy in life no matter what your circumstances or your success is. If you cannot be happy broke, you will never be happy with money and success. Find you in your life, because money and success will only amplify your personality traits or faults. Success is that elusive and almost indefinable goal to which all men are looking, but success is hardly ever the same thing to two different people. We are prone to apply the term successful to those who look prosperous or wealthy or appear to have scaled the pinnacle of accomplishment in their own profession. But is this really a success? No, I think not.

As a health professional, I am very aware that in our society men tend not to come forward for help when they experience emotional distress or discomfort. Many view it as weakness, as a sign they can't cope. They are not willing to admit to anyone, even professionals, that they feel something other than what is perceived as "normal". So, they push it away and deny their experience. No one else is talking about it, they must be the only one who feels this way. Society seems to suggest it is more natural for women to experience emotion and thus they are allowed to talk about it, but real men shouldn't cry. So, they bottle up their emotions, pretending they are not there, trying to manage them alone but with no knowledge of how to do that and no model from society of how to do so.

The gender stereotypes that are still pervasive in many western cultures play into this fear that men have of fully expressing themselves. "Don't be such a girl" and "suck it up" are among many phrases that discourage men from expressing emotion and it is most apparent in the ways we bring up our children. But for men without healthy outlets for emotion it is bottled up into helplessness or comes out as aggression because there are few other socially acceptable ways to express themselves. Men experience as many emotions as women. Our brains are similar. Yes, there are differences but the main difference in expression is one that comes from cultural and societal norms that expect men to retain a Stiff Upper Lip. As a registered nurse, I have worked in mental health services, traditional health services, penitentiaries and corporations, large and small. In all I have seen similar attitudes from men, amounting to the repression of emotion and the unwillingness to admit to distress for fear of being seen as unable to cope or weak. It is concealed under a veneer, of happiness, of love, of successful coping or even success and power. But it is there, unseen and thus unchallenged.

The added stress that comes from a high-pressure job, the responsibilities put upon an executive within a company or long hours at work away from family all play into this sense of failing to be everything you can be. Taking all this into account it's easier to relate to the pressure people can experience. Many men experiencing stress and burnout don't recognize it as such because no-one else is talking about it and it seems so commonplace in today's frenetic world, "Everyone else can cope so why can't I?" But stress is not normal, it is not how we were designed to live and the physical, mental and emotional repercussions of not dealing with the daily stress that most of us experience is detrimental to our health and well-being.

As a society, we need to encourage people to talk about stress and the more negatively perceived emotions and make it acceptable to do so. Within corporations where it is acknowledged there is a lot of pressure on employees. We need to understand that busy does not equate to productive and start being more understanding of the whole of our employees' lives. People bring their whole selves to work, and they take all the stress and difficulty of work back into their home lives. We cannot separate ourselves into distinct categories and emotions are a part of everything we do, it is unavoidable so why deny it? Is emotion an inability to cope? No, it is a natural response to life. But unexpressed; kept inside, it can become something much darker. It grows and writhes, at worst it can push people into positions where they feel unable to continue, that they are worthless and weak and that those around them would be better off if they were gone. It is not a cry for help, it is far beyond that.

Generally speaking, we are unhappy because we are dissatisfied, and this is because we pursue things that cannot make us happy, even if we obtain them. In the words of H. W. Beecher, "Success is full of promise till men get it, and then is as a last year's nest, from which the bird has flown." We exist largely disconnected from our extended families, friends and communities — except in the shallow interactions of social media — because we are too busy trying to "make it" without realizing that once we reach that goal, it won't be enough. The comedian and actor Jim Carrey talked about "getting to the place where you have everything everybody has ever desired and realizing you are still unhappy. The fact that you can still be unhappy is a shock when you have accomplished everything you ever dreamed of and more." If only we get that big raise, or a new house or have children we will finally be happy. But we won't. In fact, as Carrey points out, in many ways achieving all your goals provide the opposite of fulfillment: It lays bare the truth that there is nothing you can purchase, possess or achieve that will make you feel fulfilled over the long term. Changing our culture is critical. Being honest with others about our own personal struggles and dark nights of the soul is the first step. People on the edge need to hear stories that assure them there is a way through the all-consuming pain to a meaningful life.

As I look back on my life, I realize that happiness cannot be worked for or planned for. It comes to us like a cool breeze on a hot summer day. We must enjoy it while it is there, because often it passes on and cannot be recaptured. Now, at my time of life, happiness is in the present, to be made the most of and relished to the full; every hour, every gesture of friendship, is precious and means happiness. I believe that if we could only realize when we are young that happiness is relishing every moment as it comes, we might realize true happiness in our lifetime and stop searching for it.

CHAPTER NINE

The Perils of Telling A Single Story

I recently connected with a friend (for the purpose of this narrative, I will call John), whom I had not seen in over 20 years. During our meeting, we discussed the event that preceded our separation. Now, more than 20 years later, as I reflect on this situation, I realize the lessons and values in what I will phrase "the perils of telling a single story." Several years ago, a message had been conveyed to me that upon later review, was never relayed by John. However, I did not seek the authenticity of the story but rather, accepted it for what it was. In my mind, I expected John to volunteer the truth to me. But as I found out (these many years later), John was not to be bothered by the fact that I chose to believe a single story; that I made no effort whatsoever to first verify the story but chose to believe and act on it. All I knew about the situation was what had been conveyed to me and by hearing it over and over, it become impossible for me to see him as anything else but this. That was my single story of my friend John.

As I reflect on this situation, I realize how wrong I was to have expected him to tell his own story. After hearing the accusations, I could simply have made him aware of the messages and waited for a response, if he wanted to respond. I should have given him the opportunity to tell his story from his perspective, but I did not. When asked why he did not volunteer to offer his perspective, John replied that he would have told me what I wanted to hear because that is what I wanted to hear. My whole-body language he said, believed what I had heard so what was the point of telling his side of the story, I would never believe him. My actions had spelt it all out, he was guilty, so why would he bother to prove his innocence. What he said he found disappointing was the fact that with my education, I had convicted him without a trial. Today, more than 20 years from this incident as I reconnected with John, I realize the perils of telling a single story. I realize that every story has multiple stories depending on who tells the story, how the story is told, to whom the story is told and how they talk about the story. John challenged me to reflect on my actions after hearing his story from other people.

As an educator, I try to instill in my students the perils of a telling a single story. Failing to do so in my opinion is a disservice to students. For why would we encourage a narrow view of the world so much so that when students hear a single story, they act on it without questioning the story. Why would we judge and accuse others based on a single story? Why would we teach students not to know that a story, even a written story is as good as the one who is saying it, the one who is writing it and the one who forwards it? I make every effort to instill in my students the ability to think differently and to know that every story has multiple faces and that they should never use one story to form an opinion or decision about anything.

We are all vulnerable in the face of a single story. I recall my experience when I attended university. My roommate was shocked by me and asked where I had learned to speak English so well and was confused when I said that English was the official language in my country. He asked if he could listen to what he called my "tribal music," and was consequently very disappointed when I produced my tape of Mariah Carey. What struck me was this: He had felt sorry for me even before he saw me. His default position toward me, was a kind of patronizing, well-meaning, pity. My roommate had a single story of Africa. A single story of catastrophe. In this single story there was no possibility of Africans being similar to him, in any way. No possibility of feelings more complex than pity. No possibility of a connection as human equals. Now, after more than half of my life spent in the U.S, I can understand my roommate's response to me. If I had not grown up in Africa, and if all I knew about Africa were from popular images in the media, I too would think that Africa was a place of beautiful landscapes, beautiful animals, and incomprehensible people, fighting senseless wars, dying of poverty and AIDS, unable to speak for themselves, and waiting to be saved, by a kind, white foreigner. Looking at the media today, I begin to realize that my roommate must have, throughout his life, seen and heard different versions of this single story.

But I must quickly add that I too am just as guilty in the question of the single story. A few years ago, I visited South America. The political climate in the U.S. at the time was tense. And there were debates going on about immigration. And, as often happens in America, immigration becomes synonymous with Mexicans. There were endless stories of Mexicans as people who were fleecing the healthcare system, sneaking across the border, being arrested at the border. I remember walking around on my first day watching people going to work, rolling up tortillas in the marketplace, smoking, laughing. I remember first feeling slight surprise. And then I was overwhelmed with shame. I realized that I had been so immersed in the media coverage of Mexicans that they had become one thing in my mind, the abject immigrant. I had bought into the single story of Mexicans and I could not have been more ashamed of myself. So that is how to create a single story, show a people as one thing, as only one thing, over and over again, and that is what they become. As a child, I experienced the joys of a happy childhood, full of laughter and love in a very close-knit family. But I also experienced death, and inadequate healthcare, and repressive governments. All of these stories make me who I am. But to insist on only those negative stories is to flatten my experience, and to overlook the many other stories that formed me. The single story creates stereotypes. And the problem with stereotypes is not that they are untrue, but that they are incomplete. They make one story become the only story.

I've always felt that it is impossible to engage properly with a place or a person without engaging with all of the stories of that place and that person. The consequence of the single story is this: It robs people of dignity. It makes our recognition of our equal humanity difficult. It emphasizes how we are different rather than how we are similar. So, what if before my Mexico trip I had followed the immigration debate from both sides, the U.S. and Mexico? What the Nigerian writer Chinua Achebe calls "a balance of stories." What if my roommate knew about my neighbor, a remarkable man who left his job in a bank to follow his dream and start a publishing house? What if my roommate knew about my friend Dr. Ampoumah, a fearless man who hosts a radio show and is determined to tell the stories that we prefer to forget? What if my roommate knew about contemporary African music? Talented people singing mixing influences from Jay-Z to Bob Marley. What if my roommate knew about the female lawyer who recently went to court in Nigeria to challenge a ridiculous law that required women to get their husband's consent before renewing their passports? What if my roommate knew about Nollywood, full of innovative people making films despite great technical odds? Films so popular that they really are the best example of Africans consuming what they produce. Every time I read about Africa, I am confronted with the usual sources of irritation; the failed infrastructure, the failed government. But also, by the incredible resilience of people who thrive despite the government, rather than because of it.

It is impossible to talk about the single story without talking about power. Like economic and political worlds, stories too are defined by the principle of power. How they are told, who tells them, when they're told, how many stories are told, are really dependent on power. Power is the ability not just to tell the story of another person, but to make it the definitive story of that person. What we all must realize is that there is no single story to every story. Each of us chooses how to tell a story and we must choose never to listen to a single story. There are, in each story, different versions of the story.

Stories matter. Many stories matter. Stories have been used to dispossess and to malign. But stories can also be used to empower, and to humanize. Stories can break the dignity of a people. But stories can also repair that broken dignity. The American writer Alice Walker wrote this about her southern relatives who had moved to the north. She introduced them to a book about the southern life that they had left behind. "They sat around, reading the book themselves, listening to me read the book, and a kind of paradise was regained." When we reject the single story, we realize that there is never a single story about any place, we regain a kind of paradise. What is fascinating is that, nowadays, the media has been awash with information of single stories of people that are written and shared on their behalf by other people who make the stories. What is more disturbing is that when these stories are written or shared, there are those who believe them as they are and act on them. There are those who choose to be vulnerable in the face of a single story. Do you believe that a woman was ever stripped naked simply because you received a Facebook video or WhatsApp message? Or do you believe it because you saw it or you verified the information or you talked to the woman? An in-depth analysis of the media reveals that we have fallen into the trap of a single story. We need to beware of a single story, for in believing it, we rob ourselves of the ability to make and remake ourselves for the better.

CHAPTER TEN

Ever Felt Like a Phony in Your Own Life? Why Feeling Like a Fraud Can Be a Good Thing

No matter what stage I'm at in life, I've never been able to shake the feeling that I'm one test result, class admission or promotion away from being caught out and revealed to be a charlatan. Underlying this is a feeling that everyone else belongs or is more worthy. Other people deserve their position in a creative writing class, or in the hierarchy of the working world, perceived or otherwise, while I'm bragging my way, convinced I'm going to be called out at the next brainstorming meeting: " Jonas, we're very important people and you just don't fit in. Please take your laptop, outlandish ideas and bare-faced sham elsewhere".

These irrational thoughts aren't uncommon. The feeling of unmerited acknowledgement is called "Impostor Syndrome" and if you suffer from it too, you are in good company. In the Charisma Myth, Olivia Fox Cabane writes that she always asks her class at Stanford Business School: "How many of you in here feel that you're the one mistake the Admissions Committee made?" Each year, roughly two-thirds of the class raise their hands. This despite the fact that they've all overcome significant hurdles, requiring both hard work and talent, to get there. It explains why I used to take a ruler with me to get my exam results in college. I'd repeatedly line up the marks with my name, thinking I'd somehow made a mistake.

If you feel inadequate or that you are likely to be "found out" at work, you're probably not alone. The phenomenon called the "impostor syndrome" is very common. The novelist Maya Angelou once said, "I have written 11 books but each time I think 'Uh-oh, they're going to find out now, I've run a game on everybody, and they're going to find me out." Angelou was nominated for the Pulitzer Prize, and won five Grammys for her spoken recordings, plus a myriad other award. But the "impostor syndrome" - had her firmly in its grip. Public acclaim didn't dent the feeling that, deep down, she was a fraud, who didn't have a clue what she was doing. Think about that for a minute. Despite winning Grammys and being nominated for a Pulitzer Prize, this huge talent still questioned her success.

You've probably felt the same. Most of us have. Yet a crucial element of the impostor phenomenon is the sense that you're the only person to suffer. So, you may not find it reassuring to learn that Angelou felt it too. "Sure," you tell yourself, "she thought she was a fraud - but I really am one. And any day now, I'll be rumbled." But the truth is you're far from the only sufferer. I have discovered the impostor phenomenon lurking in the minds of authors, artists, musicians, businesspeople - even a brain surgeon. "Part of you knows you're not as good as you're pretending to be," says Henry Marsh, a neurosurgeon and author of the memoir Do No Harm. "But you have to come across as being relatively competent and confident."

Author Frances Hardinge won the 2015 Costa Book of the Year Award for her novel The Lie Tree - but still, she says, with every new project, there's a "part of my brain that tells me that this is the book... where I disappoint everybody, and people see me for the fraud I am." The underlying fear, says artist and musician Amanda Palmer, "is that someone's going to come knocking at the door. They feel that they've somehow managed to slip through the system undetected [so] in their mind it's just a matter of time before they're found out. Perhaps the most frustrating irony is that getting better at your job won't make the phenomenon go away. The more knowledge you acquire, the higher corporate levels you reach, the more likely you are to find yourself in new terrain - and therefore feeling like you're winging it.

The ultimate explanation for the impostor phenomenon lies in a fundamental fact about the human mind: we only know what's going on inside our own heads. We hear our own constant monologue of self-doubt, but never anyone else's - making it all too easy to assume that nobody else has one. As the saying goes, we "compare our insides with other people's outsides" and judge ourselves lacking as a consequence. The phenomenon seems to be ever more relevant in today's hyper-competitive, economically insecure world. It's a problem rendered more acute by social media, which encourages us to present to the world a "highlights reel" of our lives, rather than the messy psychological reality.

So now that we know its name and that other people deal with it too, our next step is to understand why we feel this way. I think part of the impostor syndrome comes from a natural sense of humility about our work. That's healthy, but it can easily cross the line into paralyzing fear. When we have a skill or talent that has come naturally, we tend to discount its value. Why is that? Well, we often hesitate to believe that what's natural, maybe even easy for us, can offer any value to the world. In fact, the very act of being really good at something can lead us to discount its value. But after spending a lot of time fine-tuning our ability, isn't it sort of the point for our skill to look and feel natural?

All of this leads to the most important step: learning how to live with the impostor syndrome. In her book "Radical Acceptance" Tara Brach shares a cool story about Buddha and the demon Mara. One day, Buddha was teaching a large group, and Mara was moving around the edges, looking for a way into the group. I envision Mara rushing frantically back and forth in the bushes and trees, making plans to wreak havoc. One of Buddha's attendants saw Mara, ran to Buddha and warned him of Mara's presence. Hearing his attendant's frantic warning, the Buddha simply replied, "Oh good, invite her in for tea." This story captures beautifully how we should respond to the impostor syndrome. We know what the feeling is called. We know others suffer from it. We know a little bit about why we feel this way. And we now know how to handle it: Invite it in and remind ourselves why it's here and what it means.

Is there any hope of escaping these ever-present feelings of fraudulence?

- Talking openly about the problem is a start. But it's also a matter of "changing your thoughts, slowly over time", and taking risks in spite of the inner voice telling you you'll fail.
- Do the thing that scares the heck out of you, realize you survived - or maybe you fell flat on your face. But you gave it your best shot."
- You don't need to try to eradicate the impostor feelings - but you also don't need to obey them, either.
- Ultimately, you should probably worry more if someone tells you they've never felt like a fraud. These ultra-confident people may simply be too incompetent to realize how incompetent they are.

This cognitive bias is known as the Dunning-Kruger effect, and the classic example concerns a bank robber who was astonished to be caught despite having smeared lemon juice on his face, which he believed made him invisible to security cameras. It was an idiotic belief, of course - but he was too much of an idiot to see it. The truly incompetent, in short, rarely worry about being truly incompetent. And this logic has a reassuring flipside for anyone grappling with impostorism: if you're sufficiently self-aware to worry that you might be a fraud... you may well not be.

For me, even after 12 years or teaching and public speaking all over the world, you think I'd be used to it. In fact, the impostor syndrome has not gone away, but I've learned to think of it as a friend. So now when I start to hear that voice in my head, I take a deep breath, pause for a minute, put a smile on my face and say, "Welcome back old friend. I'm glad you're here. Now, let's get to work."

CHAPTER ELEVEN

From Passion to Action: The Joy of Volunteerism and How it Elevated My Career

We see people volunteering all the time. Whether they're visiting the elderly, delivering meals, stuffing envelopes and more. It's obvious that volunteering helps an individual, group or organization. But let's face it— volunteering also helps volunteers themselves. When asked the question "Why do you volunteer?" Many people refer to the old adage, "Doing good is its own reward". Many state the main reason they volunteer is because it makes them feel good. They speak of giving back for all the blessings they've been given in life. Some volunteer because they are able to, and they want to help people less able. Others speak of paying it forward—doing good things so that if they are in need, someone might help them. Other more insightful and philosophical reasons are: giving hope and inspiration to those in need; showing people that there are others who care about them; and showing that there can be something good that comes out of an unfortunate situation.

While these are valid and practical reasons, they do not go far enough. The process of volunteering itself enables the individual to gain experience that they may not get elsewhere, such as building their confidence and self-esteem. Two innate qualities that motivate someone to volunteer are — an attitude to learn and experience new things, and a willingness to share one's experiences and knowledge. Volunteering gives you a lot in return. It is all about the joy of making a difference on the one side, while receiving immense value on the other from the experience of volunteering, meeting people and learning something new.

My passion for volunteering arose out of my deep interest in networking and interacting with others to solve problems. I wanted to collaborate with peers and thus develop my sphere of influence over a period of time. From my own experience, I must say that the success of volunteering is directly proportional to the time spent on improving upon the lessons learnt. I started my volunteering journey through affiliation with local professional networks. This gave me the opportunity to meet my peers, who are involved in addressing common issues and moving an agenda forward. I also learnt that the route to learning is to listen and absorb rather than talk and convey one's viewpoints. From these network associations, I learned about and acquired Fellow status in various professional associations that would help catapult my career and increase my professional visibility and credibility; Fellow of the American College of Healthcare Executives (ACHE), Distinguished Scholar & Fellow of the National Academies of

Practice (FNAP), Nurse Executive- Advanced, Board Certified (ANCC).

This brings to mind the words of Gandhiji who said, "*The best way to find yourself is to lose yourself in the service of others.*" There are many wonderful things that will never be done if you do not do them, and volunteering for me, is one such thing. Volunteering has helped me gain sound technical knowledge of relevant issues, helped me perfect my soft skills, gain confidence and credibility to make a good professional impact. Volunteering offered me the opportunity to extend my knowledgebase, to influence the direction of an organization/project, to network with other professionals & business leaders, and, perhaps most important, to have an impact on the next generation. Volunteering, be it to serve a term on a board/council, write an article or a chapter for a textbook, be a presenter or speaker at an industry meeting naturally requires additional time from one's already busy schedule. For me, though, the benefits from doing so have outweighed the efforts in that it increased my awareness of professional matters as well as being a great way to network with my peers.

I joined the Education Committee of the National Blood Clot Alliance, out of a desire to improve education on this topic and a desire to develop relationships outside of my own organization. Having always had a passion for patient education, volunteering for the Education Committee enabled me to indulge that passion and brought me in contact with many other healthcare professionals many of whom are top leaders in the profession. Volunteering to me is a great way to stay current, improve my skills, expand tool sets, and gain exposure to "a broader set of topics than one may get in their current job."

Today, more than 20 years later, when asked the reason I initially decided to volunteer and why I continue to do so, my reasons have expanded to include the following:

- *Travel opportunities*
- *Sheer enjoyment of the work*
Joy of working with a Group of talented professionals.
Maintain relationships and making new friends
Networking opportunities
- *Keeping up with practice*
- *Giving back to the profession*
- *Making a difference in the education of future healthcare professionals*

Years after initially volunteering, I find that the need to make a difference still matters, but it is the joy of the work and, especially, the people we meet that sustain us in our volunteer efforts. Many of the individuals that I have had the pleasure of serving with are exceptionally talented people. They care deeply about their work, and they challenge me to be my best. I have volunteered for multiple organizations, and the people I've met are some of the most dedicated individuals it has ever been my pleasure to know. Volunteers are individuals who have found a passion, a purpose, in their volunteer work. Through their work, they derive a sense of well-being or personal satisfaction. In short, they have found their bliss. So, let me ask you. What is your passion? What is your bliss? How will you affect the lives of future generations? Whatever it is, volunteer or support it in whatever way you are able. You'll be glad you did.

What You Gain

• *Leadership skills, such as agenda planning, delegating, strategic planning, decision making, and managing virtual teams*

• *Collaboration and communication skills, such as brainstorming, negotiating, and developing presentations*

• *Competitive advantage, by working on key issues facing the profession*

• *Important connections, through professional networking*

• *Direct, hands-on experience, in a controlled, supportive environment*

• *Continuing Professional Development (CPD) credit for certain volunteer activities*

My passion for volunteering arose out of my deep interest in networking and interacting with others to solve problems.

CHAPTER TWELVE

Beware of the Greener Grass Syndrome: Why the Grass Is Not Always Greener on the Other Side of the Fence

"If you're always looking for someone better or more perfect, you'll never be happy in any present situation."

Let me start by telling you a story about why I say the grass is not always greener on the other side. Earlier this year, I made a decision that would change the course of my life for better or worse. After 15 years in a clinical setting, I decided that it was time to make a change. I was frustrated, burnt out, and tired of working weekends, late nights, and holidays. I began to wonder if there was something else that I could be doing to make a living and started combing over job postings online. One day, I found something that I thought could work. I went into marketing. Looking back now, it is hard to picture myself selling anyone ANYTHING. After all, when I worked in a clinical setting, my role was to steer people away from services they did not need.

I would instead listen to their needs and suggest services that wouldn't require them to spend any more than necessary. And, I am not the kind of person to put an ounce of pressure on anyone. It just wasn't my style.

"Are you sure?" my mentor asked me so wanting to be supportive but knowing what was realistic. You have so many qualities, but I didn't think that a knack for sales is one of them he told me. After talking for weeks and months about my potential career change, I started to believe it was the right move. After all, if I succeeded, I would have the potential to make a lot more money than I was making. To be honest, the thought of getting a huge raise started to sound pretty darn good. So, I gave myself the green light. "You'll never know unless you try," my mentor told. AND, I DID.

I started orientation to the job and within a month has completed the classroom portion of my training. And while I thought that things were going relatively well, I could tell that something was wrong. I looked tired, stressed, and unusually miserable for days at a time. So, after several weeks of training, my mentor confronted me and asked, "What's wrong?"

"I absolutely hate it…" I responded. So, we talked for hours and tried to figure out EXACTLY what I hated about my new job. And the truth was, I hated all of it. This new job required that I call 40 people per day on the phone in an effort to set up appointments. And while I knew that ahead of time, I found that the IDEA OF IT and ACTUALLY DOING IT were two entirely different things. I HATED CALLING PEOPLE I KNEW. HE HATED CALLING PEOPLE THAT I DIDN'T KNOW. I JUST HATED CALLING PEOPLE. Period.

I hated it so much, in fact, that I didn't want to go back. We decided that it didn't make sense for me to continue. Since it was a sales job and 100 percent commission, I wasn't getting paid to be there anyway. So, the following Monday I went to my new office, packed up my belongings, and came back home.

SO, THERE I WAS. In my mid 40's, I left my stable and well-paying job in search of greener pastures. And unfortunately, the greener pastures turned out to be just an illusion, and simply out of reach for someone with my personality and temperament. And since my old employer had already hired someone else to replace me, I knew that there was no way to get my old job back. So, I decided to look for a new job, a different job. I had to figure out what my next step should be.

How many times have we heard the cliché, "The grass is greener on the other side?" While the overuse of this phrase has mostly dulled its impact, people who experience the "grass is greener syndrome" endure a significant struggle with commitment. The hallmark of the "grass is greener syndrome" is the idea that there is always something better that we are missing. It's simply the feeling that what you have, where you are, the situation you are experiencing is not as good as it might be someplace else or in some other situation. It is not necessarily a feeling of remorse but a feeling of uncertainty. A feeling that you haven't reached what you see as the maximum benefit from your current situation. Whether it is a relationship, a job, a purchase — it is the feeling that a different choice might be better. Rather than experiencing stability, security, and satisfaction in the present environment, the feeling is there is more and better elsewhere, and anything less than ideal won't do. When it's boiled down to its bare bones, grass is greener syndrome is really just an unfortunate byproduct of self-doubt. And in a time when everyone's **lives are on full display on social media**, it's even easier to fall into the trap of comparing yourself or your relationships to others.

This mindset is extremely common. In life there almost always comes at least one time where we think even for a minute that things could be better with someone or somewhere else. It's normal, and if it is a fleeting thought there is nothing to be alarmed over. It's when we start thinking about it frequently, imagining often how things might be that we should be concerned. We all question our choices — that is human — but questioning them over and over, and thinking about what else we could have done frequently, is a sign that our current situation is not right. The problem with this is that the greener grass is usually based on fantasy and fear. The fear comes from several possibilities, including fear of being trapped in commitment, fear of boredom, fear of loss of individuality, and fear of oppression. Along with these fears comes the issue of compromise. In people who fear commitment, comprising certain desires, needs, and values for the sake of the unity can feel like oppressive sacrifice. When this happens, the perception is that there is something else out there that will allow us to have all that we crave, want, and value, and that it will happen on our terms.

This is where the element of fantasy comes in, and with the fantasy comes projection. We're going to want what we don't have, and there's a fantasy that we'll get what we don't have, and that the parts that we're currently happy with won't be sacrificed in this change. However, what ends up happening is that after the "honeymoon phase" of making the change, we find ourselves wanting to flip to the other side of the fence again because we discover that there are other things that we don't have, and because the novelty of the change wears off. It ends up being true, that we always want what we don't have, even if we've already jumped the fence several times.

This is where projection comes in. When the grass is greener on the other side, we're usually (if not always) placing personal unhappiness with ourselves onto something outside of us — generally a partner, career, living environment, etc. We rely on polishing our external environment to soothe a deeper internal dissatisfaction. Though the environment changes when jumping the fence, after a brief internal high, without constant stimulation and newness, the dissatisfaction becomes the same.

I think the cliché should be changed to this: "The grass is only as green as we keep it." The grass always starts out a nice and shiny green ('honeymoon phase'), but will begin to wear a bit with use. Then, it still needs to be maintained in order to stay a nice shade of green. The dulled green (or even brown) grass on our current side of the fence would be greener if we nurture it. The shiny green grass on the other side of the fence is our wish for our internal selves — to be happy, unscathed, and fully satisfied. The truth is, as human beings, we are all in some ways less than perfect, and therefore, the shiny grass is an illusion. Our job is to keep the grass as green as possible, which may take some outside help. But no matter what, it won't remain as green as the moment we first set foot on it.

In any career, it's healthy and normal to want to grow and evolve instead of getting complacent and becoming stagnant. But there's a huge difference between seeking to improve your career and having one-sided, unspoken doubts that things could hypothetically be better — which is often one of the ways grass is greener syndrome manifests. Careers are developed over a long period of time. It is 100% natural to look at others or other people's career and pine for elements or characteristics that you wish you had in your own. It is also important to realize that there is no such thing as a perfect career or a perfect relationship and what you perceive in others is probably just a projection of what you want for yourself. It is ok to develop life and career goals but when you're scared that your present situation isn't "good enough" for the long haul and you seek to replace your current situation rather than improve it, THAT'S when grass is greener syndrome has the opportunity to really do some damage. You might start to have omnipresent doubts about your future and constantly go back and forth on **whether or not making a change is the right choice** for you.

The biggest consequence of the grass is greener syndrome is unhappiness for the individual who suffers from it. If you're always looking for someone or something better or more perfect, you'll never be happy in any present situation. Every person, every job, and every relationship all have flaws. If you can't appreciate a life with imperfections, you'll never be happy. If you're constantly seeking an undefinable version of "better," it's likely that you'll end up unhappy no matter where you are or who you are with. But, particularly in a time when everyone is so connected online it can be tempting to **pull the plug on a relationship or career** prematurely solely because you want to feel the rush of exploring something new. You just have to ask yourself: is it worth throwing away what I have to take a gamble on something unknown?

Another significant issue with grass is greener thinking is that people don't always realize that shifting to the "greener" scenario may soothe some emotional distress and fulfill some particular needs, but in so doing has now opened gaps to previous needs that were in the process of being satisfactorily met on the side of the fence they were before. For example: a person choosing between their current relationship and the relationship that looks like could solve all of the concerns with the current relationship. The current partner is a hard worker, reliable, responsible, steady, not very sexual, not very spontaneous, and so on. The grass is greener thinker finds a potential partner who is spontaneous, sexual, and brings out the fun of being less responsible, and more risky. Maybe this is the relationship they've needed all along, is the thought. What's very important in this is: This decision is being made from the perspective of having certain needs currently being met. The subconscious radar doesn't quite internalize what it would be giving up to make the change. So the feeling is that the open needs will be met, and everything will be great. However, once shifting into that new relationship, the grass is greener thinker suddenly realizes the feeling of lack of reliability, lack of stability, lack of responsibility, and so on. Suddenly the vicious cycle is reinforced, and the grass becomes greener going the other way again.

I must insert that there are certainly situations where another situation *is* a better situation than the current one (for example, a healthy relationship versus an abusive one; a job that's more fulfilling to you versus an unfulfilling job). But the "grass is greener syndrome" has its own particular presentation, primarily rooted in patterns:

• **Repetition.** A pattern in your life of constantly wanting better and repeatedly seeking change in relationships, jobs, environment.

• **Perfection.** It's one thing to go from an abusive relationship to a positively-functioning relationship, but it's another to feel that a string of functioning relationships are never good enough. There may be a search for the fantasized ideal taking place.

• **Wanting to have and eat your cake.** This is in line with the struggle of compromise. If you must have every want and perceived need that stimulates you, then it's likely that the grass will never be green enough unless you're the only one on the grass — and even then, it won't be green enough because of what may be missing from this picture.

• **Wanting to run away.** If you see a pattern of being unable to settle in one geographic place, relationship, job, etc., there are deeper reasons for this than just not being in the "right" environment.

• **Ultimate dissatisfaction.** If you enjoy constant change, and living out this sort of life, then there's technically nothing wrong with this. But if the reason for the constant change comes from repetition of dissatisfaction, and if you're looking to become more secure, stable, and settled, then this is an issue to look into. The best way to deal with the "grass is greener syndrome" is to learn the underlying reasons beyond the abstract ideas of idealizations, perfectionism, and the inability to commit. The other piece is learning how to nurture and increase connection to what's current so the relationships maintain and strengthen rather than become unsatisfying. The idea is to build an *internal* place of stability, rather than jumping around in your external life to compensate for a lack of internal stability.

So what should you do if you want to shake the eternal feeling of anticipating the bigger and better in career and personal relationships? Aside from coming up with coping strategies so you don't unhealthily compare yourself, one way to combat those feelings is by making an **active effort to be more present** and available in your current situation. The people, experiences, and energies that cross your path are there for a reason: trust that. Don't put pressure on yourself or expect things to be a certain way. Just trust. Otherwise, you get caught up in a cycle of comparison, wondering if what you have is good enough for 'forever,' when it is just about what it good for right now. That leads to anxiety and suffering. All experiences are meant to help you grow and evolve — no one knows how long that growth phase will last. Relax and let it flow."

Of course, it's important to note that sometimes, feeling like the grass might be greener on the other side is a real red flag that your current situation or career isn't the right one for you — and it's important to be honest with yourself about situation and **trust your gut instinct**. But if you think your mindset is a result of something internal that you need to work on, practicing mindfulness can help you gain some clarity. As cliché as it sounds, it's true that the grass is greener where you water it. If you spend time 'watering' the grass of your career, you can work to improve and nurture your connection, and hopefully eventually assuage any doubts you might have had.

On the other hand, if you let your doubts and fears cloud your perceptions, you might disengage and create distance from opportunities — which will only compound your concerns and make things more difficult.

All of this being said, sometimes a change is necessary. Not all scenarios are meant to be held forever. This post isn't advocating for the status quo, as much as it's advocating for you to learn about yourself more if you're noticing a pattern of grass is greener thoughts and behaviors in your life — to make educated and informed decisions about major life changes, rather than acting out an underlying pattern that is based more in fantasy than reality. In the end, is the perceived greener scenario really ever as wonderful in reality as the fantasy? Initially the grass is bright green, but then generally starts to fade with time. It's more about how you treat, maintain, and improve what you have, rather than repeatedly uprooting and starting over. Instead of seeking to migrate to better pastures, first try watering the grass in your OWN fields — you might just be surprised how much better the grass looks when it's properly nourished.

Whether you're fighting a jealous moment for the first time or you find yourself constantly beset with everyone else's green grass, here's what to do when you don't want to be jealous anymore:

Practice Gratitude: Humans are wired to be the negative as a **survival mechanism**. If you don't actively look for the positives in your life, you can quickly lose track of all you do have. And if you focus exclusively on everything that you want then you eventually cultivate an attitude of entitlement without considering what's already working in your favor. Gratitude, on the other hand, can **help you see what's working** and balance it against what appears to not be working. Start a **gratitude habit** that forces you to consider what you have going for you in every phase of your career, such as keeping a small gratitude journal at your desk or recording what you're grateful for on your calendar every day.

Determine whether or not it's a real desire: Sometimes we're jealous because we see something we are truly lacking in our lives, and that means it's time for a change. Sometimes, however, we're jealous because we simply aren't tending our own garden. Take a closer look at what's causing you to think the grass is greener somewhere else. Would you truly be happier with different responsibilities or in a different job? Or are you jealous of the person's perceived happiness, not their position? If it's the former, you know it's time to make a change. If it's the latter, you'll want to focus on your emotional intelligence and what's going on in your personal life that might encourage these feelings.

Make a plan to change or let it go: I've fallen prey to this error in judgement too many times to count — I'll let something I want fester in my dreams, but I don't actually make any plans to achieve it. Either you're willing to commit to the change that the jealousy brings, or you must let yourself let it go. You can't want to **earn your certificate** in project management but never take the course. You can't crave a college degree and never make a plan to save money or carve out the time for it. You must use your jealousy as a catalyst for making your own grass greener or as an opportunity to let go.

Use tools as a part of your plan: If you've decided that your jealousy means it's time for change, keep in mind that making a plan doesn't have to call for a huge life renovation. Making progress can be as simple as setting up an **alert for new positions** on Simply Hired so that you're notified when the opportunity comes up instead of having to seek it out yourself. Look into tools that can help you automate and track the changes you want to implement. Don't settle for watching others tend to their "career garden." Make the grass on your side greener by practicing these tips and making small changes to help you achieve your goals. If you think the grass is greener on the other side of the fence, then try watering your own lawn.

About the Author

Dr. Nguh is a Professor in the Graduate Nursing program with Walden University where he has a double appointment in the Master of Nursing and PhD in the Public Health program. Additionally, he serves as chair of dissertation committee for PhD in Public Health program. Prior to joining Walden University, Dr. Nguh was the Chair of Graduate Nursing program at Kaplan University where he oversaw the MSN program and developed the curriculum for the DNP program. Prior to that he was the Director of Nursing at the University of the District of Columbia, Washington D.C.

Dr. Nguh holds a PhD in Public Health from Walden University, a Master of Science in Nursing from the University of Dundee in the UK, a Master of Science in Healthcare Administration from Strayer University and a Bachelor of Science in Nursing from Walden University. Dr. Nguh holds numerous fellowships including the American College of Healthcare Executive, the National Academies of Practice, and certification as Nurse Executive, Advanced from the American Nurses

Credentialing Center. Dr. Nguh is a five-time national award winner for his work in community service and volunteerism. In 2015, he was honored by the National League of Nursing with the Lillian Wald Humanitarian Award, and the Outstanding Mentor Award from the Maryland Nurses Association (2015) and the Nurse of the Year Award from Nurse.com (2012). Dr. Nguh sits on several healthcare boards including the regional chapter of Nurse.com, the Maryland Nurses Association, and the American College of Healthcare Executives (National Capital Chapter).

www.ingramcontent.com/pod-product-compliance
Lightning Source LLC
Chambersburg PA
CBHW032050040426
42449CB00007B/1052